It's Not Catching

Allergies

Heinemann
LIBRARY

Angela Royston

www.heinemann.co.uk/library

Visit our website to find out more information about **Heinemann Library** books.

To order:

 Phone 44 (0) 1865 888066

 Send a fax to 44 (0) 1865 314091

 Visit the Heinemann Bookshop at www.heinemann.co.uk/library to browse our catalogue and order online.

First published in Great Britain by Heinemann Library, Halley Court, Jordan Hill, Oxford OX2 8EJ, part of Harcourt Education. Heinemann is a registered trademark of Harcourt Education Ltd.

Editorial: Sarah Eason and Kathy Peltan
Design: Dave Oakley, Arnos Design
Picture Research: Helen Reilly, Arnos Design
Artwork: Tower Designs UK Ltd
Production: Edward Moore

Originated by Dot Gradations
Printed and bound in Hong Kong and China by South China Printing Company

The paper used to print this book comes from sustainable sources.

ISBN 0 431 02143 0 (hardback)
08 07 06 05 04
10 9 8 7 6 5 4 3 2 1

ISBN 0 431 02152 X (paperback)
09 08 07 06 05
10 9 8 7 6 5 4 3 2 1

British Library Cataloguing in Publication Data
Royston, Angela
Allergies. – (it's not catching)
616.9'7

A full catalogue record for this book is available from the British Library.

Acknowledgements
The publishers would like to thank the following for permission to reproduce photographs:
AD p. **13**; Corbis/Harcourt Index pp. **4**, **29**; Getty Images/Photographers Choice/Don Klumpp p. **20**; Getty Images/Tony Garcia p. **6**; Image Source p. **8**; Phillip James Photography pp. **10**, **11**, **12**, **27**, **28**; SPL/Alex Bartell p. **15**; SPL/Andy Harmer p. **9**; SPL/Astrid & Hanns & Frieder Michler p. **17**; SPL/BSIP EDWIGE p. **24**; SPL/Conor Caffrey p. **5**; SPL/Damien Lovegrove p. **18**; SPL/Dr Jeremy Burgess p. **14**; SPL/Oscar Burriel p. **19**; SPL/Dr H. C. Robinson p. **21**; SPL/Dr P. Marazzi p. **7**; SPL/SIU p. **25**; Trevor Clifford p. **26**; Tudor Photography p. **22**.

Cover photograph reproduced with permission of Bubbles/Frans Rombout.

The publishers would like to thank David Wright for his assistance in the preparation of this book.

Every effort has been made to contact copyright holders of any material reproduced in this book. Any omissions will be rectified in subsequent printings if notice is given to the publishers.

Contents

Words written in bold, **like this**, are explained
in the Glossary.

What is an allergy?

You have an **allergy** if something makes you feel ill although it is harmless to most other people. Holding and stroking a dog or a cat does not make most people feel ill.

However, when some people are near a pet, their eyes water and they sneeze. They are **allergic** to tiny bits of dirt in the pet's fur.

Who gets allergies?

Allergies usually run in families. This means that you are more likely to be **allergic** to something if your mother or father has an allergy.

rash caused by an
allergic reaction

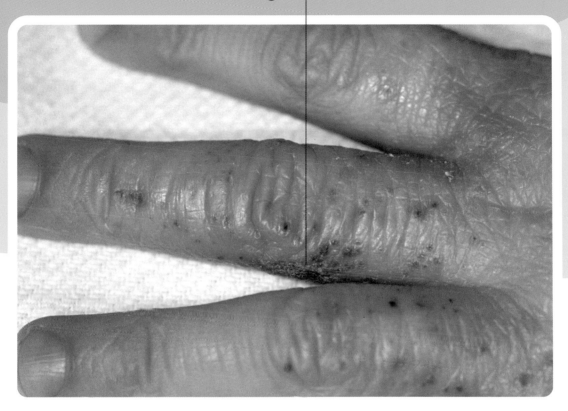

You probably will not have the same allergy
as your parents. An allergy is the way your
particular body reacts to something. You
cannot catch an allergy from someone else.

Dust and pollen

Different people are **allergic** to particular kinds of things. Some people are allergic to fine dust. The dust may come from cats, cigarettes or elsewhere.

Some people are allergic to **pollen**. Pollen is the dust that comes from grass and flowers in spring. Dust and pollen float in the air, which means that you can easily breathe them in.

Peanuts and other foods

Chinese food

peanut butter

peanut bar

salted peanuts

Some people are **allergic** to particular foods. You may be allergic to peanuts, for example. If so, you must avoid all foods that contain peanuts or peanut oils.

bread

cheese

milk

nuts

prawns

Some foods are more likely to cause **allergies** than others. The picture shows some foods that often cause allergies. Many other foods can also cause allergies.

Make-up and washing powder

Some people are **allergic** to scented soaps or other things that touch their skin. They can use special soaps and creams that do not **irritate** their skin.

Many people are allergic to the **chemicals** in **biological washing powder**. The chemicals touch their skin when they wear clothes that have been washed in the powder.

Insects and plants

Bees, wasps, fleas, dust mites and many other insects can bite or sting you. Everyone **reacts** to insect bites and stings, but some people are particularly **allergic** to them.

Many people are allergic to some plants, such as these nettles, poison ivy or to fruit trees that produce **limes**. They come out in a **rash** when the plant touches their skin.

How allergies affect people

Some people may **react** only a little bit to a particular food. Eating strawberries, for example, might make them feel a bit sick. Other people may react more strongly.

If you react strongly to strawberries, they can make you very sick. Your skin may break out in a red, itchy **rash**.

You may be **allergic** to **pollen**. If so, then you probably sneeze when the pollen **irritates** the inside of your nose. This **allergy** is called hay fever.

Hay fever can also make you cough and your nose run. Coughing and sneezing are the ways your body tries to push the pollen out of your lungs.

rashes and itchy skin

You may be **allergic** to wool or other
fabrics that you wear next to your skin.
Many **allergies** cause a **rash** and itchy skin.
Some rashes last for a few hours, others
can last longer.

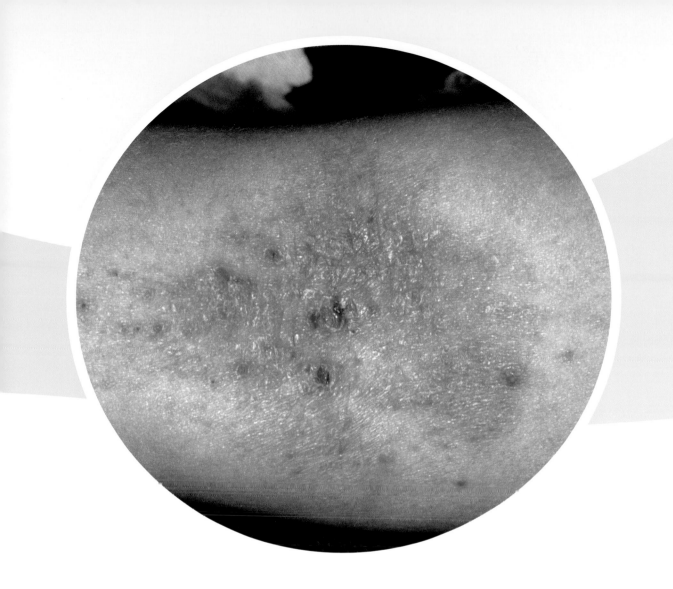

Eczema is a skin condition that many people get. It makes the skin dry and itchy. Eczema is often made worse by allergies to food, such as milk, or to scented soaps.

Vomiting and diarrhoea

If you always **vomit** after eating a particular food, you may be **allergic** to that food. Vomiting is the stomach's way of getting rid of something that **irritates** it.

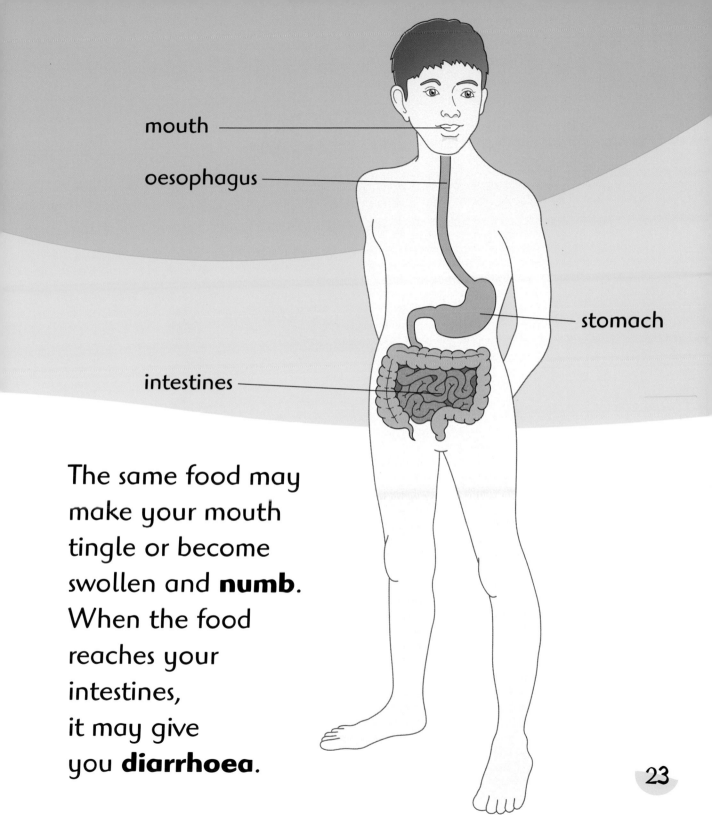

mouth

oesophagus

stomach

intestines

The same food may make your mouth tingle or become swollen and **numb**. When the food reaches your intestines, it may give you **diarrhoea**.

23

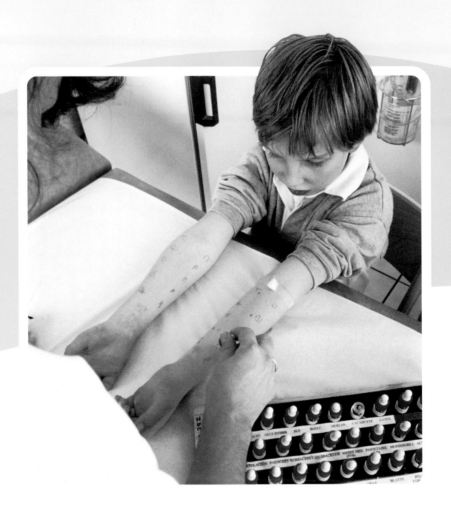

It is not always easy to tell what is causing an **allergy**. An allergy **clinic** uses special tests. Tiny amounts of different things may be put on your skin.

24

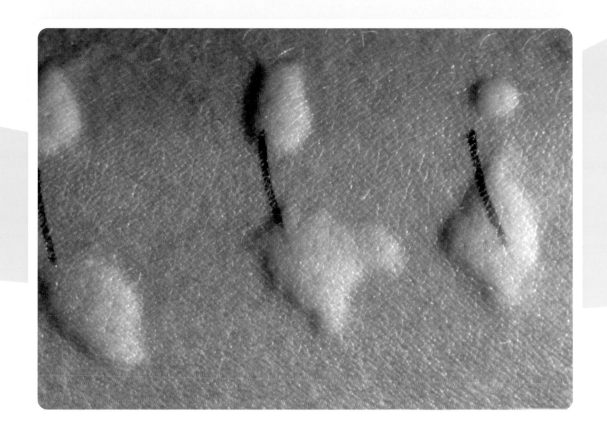

If you are **allergic**, your skin **reacts** very quickly to the thing you are allergic to. Testing a person's blood can also show up some allergies.

Treating an allergy

Different treatments help different kinds of **allergy**. The most common treatment is a medicine called **antihistamine**. It can be used as a spray, a cream or a tablet.

People who have **eczema** rub special cream into their skin. The cream soothes the skin and makes it less dry. Many children become less **allergic** as they grow older.

The best way to prevent an **allergic** reaction is to avoid the thing you are allergic to. If you are allergic to chocolate, you must not eat any chocolate.

People who are allergic to dust use special vacuum cleaners to clean their homes. Some people have to **filter** the air in their home to remove all the dust.

Glossary

allergic   having an allergy

allergy   condition when the body reacts to something as though it were harmful, although the same thing is harmless to most people

antihistamine   medicine used to treat an allergy

clinic   medical centre

biological washing powder   washing powder that contains chemicals called enzymes

chemical   a substance

diarrhoea   tummy upset when the solid waste that leaves your body when you go to the toilet is loose and runny

eczema   skin condition in which a patch or patches of skin are dry and itchy

fabric   cloth

filter   fine sieve for catching dust or other solids

hay fever   allergy to pollen

irritate make part of the body itchy or sore

limes sour green fruits a bit like lemons

numb without feeling

pollen fine dust produced by flowering plants, particularly grasses, some trees and all flowers

rash small, red spots that suddenly appear on the skin

react respond to something

vomit be sick

More books to read

Body Matters: Why Do My Eyes Itch? And Other Questions About Allergies, Angela Royston, (Heinemann Library, 2002)

Look After Yourself: Keep Healthy! Angela Royston, (Heinemann Library, 2003)

What Does It Mean To Have Allergies? Louise Spilsbury, (Heinemann Library, 2001)

Index